WINNING

THE CHANGING IMAGE OF WOMEN IN SPORTS

WOMEN

Photographs by
Tony Duffy

Text by
Paul Wade

Times
BOOKS

Published by TIMES BOOKS, a division of
Quadrangle/The New York Times Book
Co., Inc. Three Park Avenue, New York,
N.Y. 10016

Published simultaneously in Canada by
Fitzhenry & Whiteside, Ltd., Toronto

Conceived, designed and produced by
Breslich & Foss, 43 Museum Street,
London WC1A 1LY

Photographs copyright © 1983 by Tony
Duffy

Text and design copyright © 1983 by
Breslich & Foss

Library of Congress Catalog Number
82-74261
International Standard Book Number
0-8129-1069-9

82 83 84 85 86 5 4 3 2 1

Filmset by Babel Translations and Electronic
Village, London

Colour Originations by Dot Gradations,
Essex

Printed in Belgium by Brepols

CONTENTS

PROFILE OF TONY DUFFY

'I see a lot of different sports, and in the last ten years the women have got a lot better, believe me. I have always enjoyed taking photos of female athletes, too. They've got natural grace and tend to show their emotions more than the men. As a result, they're often more fun to watch.'

Tony Duffy is one of the world's leading sports photographers and a familiar sight at major sports events. As the official photographer for both the International Amateur Athletic Federation (IAAF) and the International Swimming Association (FISA) his skill is recognized by the officials of many leading Olympic events.

Tony has taken dramatic pictures at the trackside in Munich, Montreal and Moscow, and been sprayed by enthusiastic swimmers in California, Berlin and Guayaquil. But not every venue is romantic. 'In order to capture a skier silhouetted against the sky, I have to dig myself into the snow and anticipate that split second when the competitor appears at 75 mph. The cold's intense and the slopes icy. You have to understand sport, have a sympathy for it so that you can understand where the most dramatic moment will take place. Then you have to have lightning reflexes.'

One of Tony's greatest skills is knowing where to be and when to be there. At track events his carrot red hair is not always to be seen in the throng of photographers at the tape, but is often near the final bend, 'I know it's there that the athletes make their final burst of effort into the finishing straight. That's when everyone in the race is digging deep into their reserves of strength and courage, so that's where the best pictures are frequently to be had.'

Taking top class photographs in any field requires not only technical expertise, but enthusiasm and sympathy. Tony took the picture of Janet Pinneau in Chapter 4 walking along a beach in California. 'I saw this girl practising and thought 'Hey, she's really good'.' She turned out to be a star softball catcher and Tony arranged an impromptu photo session there and then. Such enthusiasm, though, is tempered with an understanding of the pressure facing any sports star today. It is as important to know when to take a picture as when not to take one. 'Surprising as some photographers find it, 'says Tony, 'there are times when the last thing a sportsman or woman wants to see is the lens of a camera pointing at them.' It is an attitude that has led to friendships with many sports personalities.

Since setting up as a specialist sports photographer in 1972, Tony has won a sparkling array of awards and prizes, including the Sports Photographer of the Year (1975) and the International Sports Photo of the Year (1975, 1977 and 1981). His London agency, All-Sport, houses his unique collection of old sports photographs and acts as a base for Tony and his staff to travel to events all over the world.

THE REVOLUTION

'Even the most uncompromising champion of the rights and capacities of women must admit that in contests of physical skill, speed and endurance they must remain forever the weaker sex.'

The London *Daily News* published this passage in an editorial on 6 August 1926. On the same day a 19-year-old New Yorker, Gertrude Ederle, became the first woman to swim the English Channel and she did it in a faster time than any man had done before.

The myth that sporting women 'must remain forever the weaker sex' endured until the 1970s when their triumphs became a regular feature of the daily news. Today, top sports trainers like Gordon Richards point out that 'it is only elite men who can hold off the challenge of the fitter, better-trained, better-coached women.' In fact, some research (particularly by Dr K.F.Dyer in *Catching up the Men*) forecasts that women will not only equal men's performances in some sports in the future, but overtake them. In the struggle for 'sports lib', women are winning.

Surprisingly, however, the Feminist, or Women's Liberation Movement has taken little interest in leisure issues. It identifies the main 'problem' areas as education, work and housework and has virtually ignored female involvement in sport. Perhaps that is why sportswriters still thrive on copy dotted with epithets like 'petite blonde', 'bright-eyed', 'attractive brunette' and 'sexy'. Observant writers like Paul Gallico—'Never saw a good lady swimmer with small feet' — are few and far between.

Track and Field Athletics
IRIS DAVIS
USA

'It is only the elite men who can hold off the challenge of the fitter, better-trained, better-coached women.'

The potential of women in sport seems to be governed more by attitude of mind than by strength of body. Dr Don Anthony, a sport and physical education expert at London's Avery Hill College, writes:

The difficulties which women still face in achieving full emancipation in sport are partly linked to ritual behaviour. Some of the reasons advanced for limiting women to certain sports activities are astonishing. It was not many years ago that I read articles by eminent psychologists stating that kicking was not in woman's true nature! Unmarried psychologists undoubtedly. It is interesting to consider the ways in which women might invade traditionally male sports in the future. There are no valid reasons why women do not pole-vault and throw the hammer in athletics. Both events are more graceful and less strenuous than shot-putting. Women with the gymnastic ability evident in the asymmetrical bars find pole-vaulting easy and enjoyable. They also find satisfaction in the techniques of hammer-throwing, which uses the whole body in a rhythmic and balanced way. Of course a lighter hammer is needed. Women are already playing football. The best women in swimming and track and field athletics are better than good men. When women have been allowed to train with men and according to the same principles, their performances have soared—this is one of the reasons for their success in East Germany. Mixed events are traditional in tennis, they are growing in golf. I can see no reason why mixed relays should not be commonplace in swimming and athletics. Basketball and volleyball are transformed and given a more sensitive quality, yet are still realistic, when played with mixed teams.

Even if men can be persuaded that sport and women are totally compatible, women themselves still have problems in understanding their relatively new role as competitors. Dr Letha Hunter, a sports medicine expert in Atlanta, Georgia told *The New York Times*: 'A guy who competed and won proved his masculinity, a woman who did the same thing had to prove her femininity. Once if you were a 6-foot girl you were an oddball, you hunkered down. Now you're looked on with admiration and offered a [college athletic] scholarship. That's a psychological adaptation and it had to come first.'

The barrier to women's success in sport then is too often a psychological one, foisted on them over the centuries. They were simply not supposed to be active in sport. For years mothers worried about daughters who showed hearty sporty tendencies. They called them 'tomboys', applauded them at 8, 9 or 10, but became anxious when they reached their teens. Educational psychologists now support what former tomboy Billie Jean King asserts, 'Athletics are an essential part of education for both sexes. Girls and boys are going to grow up easier in each other's company.'

This has been difficult in Western countries, especially the USA, where sport and masculinity go hand in hand. Boys were encouraged to take part in sports, girls were expected to play with dolls and help around the house. Their participation was limited to cheerleading or applauding from the stands. Although girls develop more quickly than boys in their early years, the fact that they were (and often still are) steered towards non-sporting activities has been revealed as harmful. Girls need to play in order to continue the learning process begun as a baby. From crawling to running, from manipulating an object to throwing it, catching and balancing, all these physical skills need to be developed if they are to be readily available later. Give a girl a chance to play, a chance to educate her body and she will enjoy life more fully. The mother of American basketball player Nancy Lieberman admitted that she 'always wanted a little girl who wore dresses and played with dolls' but that, having a daughter who won an Olympic silver medal, she was 'not complaining'.

However, the greatest pressure on sportswomen can come from their mothers. British Olympic Association doctor and sports medicine expert Malcolm Read finds this to be an increasing problem. 'You see most girls pushed in gymnastics. Certainly in Britain I spend so much time having to hold back parents, while I try to find out what the girl actually wants to do. On a couple of occasions I've told the mother that when I'm examining her daughter's injury I'll either say "we're going to give you some physiotherapy" and scratch my nose at the same time, or merely say "we're going to give you treatment". Girls often *claim*

that they're injured in order to get out of doing the sport because they're being pressured. If I find that there's no injury, then I scratch my nose. Then, I talk to the girl and hope to find out in the course of conversation that she is not really injured. Then I have to persuade the parents that they are overdoing it.'

On the other hand Malcolm Read applauds the growing awareness in women of all ages that exercise is not only good for them, but is fun too. 'When I coach youngsters I always insist that they stay around after a practice session to chat. Sport is a great mixer.' In Britain and the USA where socializing seems to be getting more difficult in urban areas, the idea of meeting and making friends while out hiking or jogging or swimming is far more attractive and sensible than sitting in a singles bar. For a start, there must be a common interest. Exercise classes or bingo? Squash or coffee mornings? Tennis or a Tupperware party? Women are showing their preference more and more. In 1970 so few women went jogging that it was rated at zero; twelve years later one third of the 17 million joggers in the USA were estimated to be women. Now there is a 'can do' attitude, typified by the New Zealand archer Neroli Fairhall. She lost the use of her legs in a motorcycle accident in 1969 and has been confined to a wheelchair ever since. In October 1982 she won the gold medal at the Commonwealth Games in Brisbane, Australia in competition against ablebodied women. This is the first time a paraplegic has won a major title in open competition. Asked if she thought she had an advantage in shooting from a seated position, Fairhall replied, 'I can't answer that. I've never shot standing up.'

The sheer prudery of a male dominated society has been one of the principal factors affecting women's attitude to sport, as well as women's success in sport. When women's bodies had to be totally enveloped in clothing, even a brisk walk must have been a strain. The popularity of a genteel game like croquet was enhanced a century ago by women who had the temerity to expose their ankles. The bicycle was even more effective, as American feminist leader Elizabeth Cady Stanton pointed out in 1888, 'Many a woman is riding to suffrage on a bicycle.' When Suzanne Lenglen burst on the tennis scene after World War I, her sheer athleticism demanded release from the constrictions of long dresses and even hats. Wearing a one-piece cotton frock, she was described as 'shocking' and 'indecent' because her skirt reached only to mid-calf. But she won Wimbledon six times.

Women were similarly restricted in swimming. The heavy black knitted wool suit made a swimmer look more like a large dog than an athlete. Stockings were sometimes required, and even after World War II, a prim little 'skirt' was considered an essential part of a swimsuit. Ironically, it was the supposedly liberated teenage Americans who were shocked by the revealing second-skin suits worn by the East German girl swimmers in 1973.

Even today traditional ideas of propriety are sometimes contrary to all acknowledged medical expertise. Britain's Lesley Watson, a veteran of some 70 marathons was criticized for having a string-type ventilation around the midriff of her running vest in 1982. Not surprisingly, she was furious. As a physiotherapist she is well aware of the dangers of the body overheating when running 26 miles in the summer. Official excitement over the glimpse of a bra was petty to say the least, especially as it was the *women's* athletics association that was upset.

A popularly recorded breakthrough involves a woman who has been effective in liberating women in sport, Kathrine Switzer. She now runs the Avon Cosmetics sports program, having worked her way up the hard way. In a well-publicised incident in the 1967 Boston Marathon, Switzer was almost thrown out of the race by its Scottish-American organiser, Jock Semple. In those days, women were not allowed to run further than 800 metres in competition on the track, so the idea of covering 26 miles 385 yds was totally unacceptable. Luckily, Switzer's boyfriend at that time was a muscular shotputter and he bounced Semple out of the way so that she could continue the race. Her success in completing the distance opened a floodgate that is still producing a torrent of talented runners.

Perhaps the most noticeable development has been the boom in media interest. When the advertising executives of Madison Avenue saw a new way of exploiting 50 per cent of their market, they grabbed on to the shirtails of women's professional sport, sweat and all. Unwittingly, they did women a good turn at the same time. Television commercials began to use Chris Evert to sell cosmetics and shampoos. The Bonne Bell company used the image of a woman jogger to promote healthy perspiration and backed their campaign by sponsoring sports events. Even models themselves looked less pale and soignée, preferring to look as if their swimsuits actually got wet.

The effect of sponsorship and prize money on women's sports has been dramatic. Even though the US Professional Women's Bowling Association dates back to 1959, it was not until the tennis players followed the men's lead and organized a pro circuit in 1970 that professional women's sports took off. Virginia Slims cigarettes invested $40,000 in women's tennis and continue to collect on their gamble. Colgate, through pressure from their British chief executive David Foster, put money in women's golf; the prize fund has grown steadily ever since. In 1975, there was $1.2 million in prize money; in 1982 it was $6.4 million. Furthermore, many professionals suggest that the average male golfer would learn more from watching the women pros that the men. Top men can accelerate the clubhead to a blurring speed, an example that most people cannot copy. By contrast, women like Nancy Lopez have a commendable rhythm and this helps them to outdrive most men in the high handicap divisions.

Professional women's sport has been a great example to girls and women all over the world. But that does not mean that the professionals have pleased the feminist movement. Women's golf in the USA used sex appeal to promote the sport and succeeded in drawing crowds, TV and money to their circuit. It was an advertising man, Ray Volpe, who persuaded the LPGA that they needed a more glamorous image to catch up with the paypackets earned by women tennis players. He used a blonde called Laura Baugh as the bait for the men of the media. And it worked. Even though Baugh never won a tournament, she gave the reporters and their cameramen the glamour they wanted. Now Jan Stephenson of Australia does the same job, but she is also a winner which makes even more of an impact. Without them, JoAnne Carner would not have amassed the million dollars in prize money that she earned in 1981. Known as Big Momma because of her solid build and equally solid driving power, she has a dry sense of humour and wears a golfing visor promoting refrigerators where the more glamorous touring pros advertise lingerie.

The success of touring professionals may be calculated each week in dollars, but the price women have had to pay emotionally is still difficult to estimate. Carner is lucky to have been married for eighteen years to a man affluent enough to be able to accompany her on the long, arduous circuit whose sponsors demand that the stars attend every tournament.

One of the spin-offs of the promotional razzmatazz accompanying the marriage of big business and sport is that it intensifies the spotlight on individual stars. In some cases this can be greatly to the advantage of the sport, and both the tennis and golf pro circuits have benefited from the wide range of characters that have emerged. Indeed, if one figure can be singled out for her contribution to breaking down barriers between men and women in sport, it is the American tennis player Billie Jean King. Her campaigning over the last fifteen years has shown both men and women that female competitors can provide all the excitement, skill, guts and showbiz that the males can.

'Sometimes there are moments when I feel unimportant,' said King, 'I think, sport—big deal! But what is sport anyway? An art, an amusement. We professionals are the motivators, we're the ones who inspire. We give people something they have for the rest of their lives. They're better in health, mind and spirit. So I do contribute. I give people pleasure and happiness.'

As a contrast to the ebullient Billie Jean King, tennis has also had the quiet wit and graceful poise of Chris Evert Lloyd. Highly competitive ('The winning, I always liked the winning'), she was long regarded as the typical girl-next-door, even though she pleaded for a more grown-up image. 'It would be very nice if some writer would get around to describing me as sexy.'

In the amateur world, another woman who influenced millions also suffered from the 'little girl' image. In 1972, the press and the television picked out Olga Korbut as the star of the Munich Olympics. Olga won three gold and one silver medal, but it was her perkiness that caught the audience and won their hearts. She started an avalanche of interest in gymnastics in the Western world that gave schoolgirls a chance to enjoy a sport that did not require them to spend afternoons in the rain on hockey or lacrosse fields. In 1982, British gymnastic official Tony Murdoch estimated that even if a new club opened every day of the year, there would still not be enough room to contain the enthusiasts for the sport.

Iceskating, like gymnastics, has for long been readily acceptable to large portions of the general public. Girls who followed Korbut's example of playing to the audience have at times made this sport seem a part of the entertainment world. Unlike the gymnasts, iceskaters have a tradition of winning Olympic and World titles and then turning professional. Sonja Henie of Norway earned an estimated $47,500,000 in her career, which included several movies. As a sports star she outearned everyone until Muhammad Ali. But although Hollywood capitalised on the success of sports celebrities such as swimmer Esther Williams, they were scarcely stars with whom the cinema-goers could really identify.

Less immediately noticeable than the media and business interest in sportswomen, but nonetheless important, is the sports rivalry between America and the Soviet bloc countries. When Eastern European nations, especially the Soviet Union, began to dominate women's events at the Olympic Games, the Americans realized that natural ability and amateur attitudes were no longer enough to ensure victory in the 'Cold War Games'.

In 1968, America's track and field women had disastrous results in the Mexico Olympics, winning a mere four medals out of a possible thirty-six. In the battle for supremacy between the political opponents of East and West, the message filtered through that America's women had to be given more practical help and Title IX (Title Nine) was born. Congress passed Title IX of the Education Amendments, providing that 'no person in the United States shall, on the basis of sex, be excluded from participation in any program or activity receiving federal financial assistance...' It took some time for this decision to be interpreted intelligently. Did it mean that women should be allowed to try out for the football team? Should they be allowed equal time in the college gymnasium or swimming pool? Should they be offered an equal number of athletic scholarships? And should they have as much money lavished on them as men?

Test cases began to hit the headlines. In 1973 in New Jersey the courts ruled that girls should be allowed to play Little League baseball. Male chauvinists shuddered, complaining that the American way of life was at risk. In 1974, the Little League itself changed its rules to allow girls to play.

Suddenly, successful competitors were being recruited by American colleges and offered scholarships. Women's sports were on the map. Arizona State, for example, has a synchronised swimming program, coached by Kathy Kretschmer who says that 'synchro swimming was a hometown sport until 1972, when Title IX came in.' Now it is an Olympic sport.

The assistance that women were receiving in the USA was noticed by European countries who were also organizing their amateur athletics. As the 1970s progressed, women began to make their mark in all sorts of sports. Horse-racing, so long a male bastion both on and off the track, accepted women as both trainers and jockeys. Experts say that they have 'sensitive hands and are particularly good at introducing two-year-old fillies to racing and at riding sour or nervous horses.' They suffer fewer weight problems than men do, but are thought to be at a disadvantage in strong finishes since they are not as strong pound for pound. A Welsh girl, Joanna Morgan, must take particular satisfaction at having beaten the great Lester Piggott in a photo-finish. And French jockeys were taken aback when Britain's Janet Slade beat them in a steeplechase! In Europe, where the winter months are dedicated to steeplechasing and hurdling, women seem to be more competitive than in the summer's flat racing. This can be traced to the traditional equality that women have had on the hunting field. Writing in 1885, the Duke of Beaufort was grudgingly appreciative of the same skills that are apparent a century later:

How often we hear a woman praised for hands; how often we hear it said that the gentler sex have naturally better hands than we men. Partly, no doubt, this is because they are the 'gentler sex', because they have not the strength to pull and haul a horse about that we, alas! have. But mainly it comes from this, that they are content to leave their horses alone. Mounted, as they mostly are, and certainly always should be, on thoroughly trained and experienced hunters, they are satisfied to leave everything to the horse; it is his business to carry them; theirs to be carried. Whether this happy state of confidence arises from their superior tact, or from ignorance, matters nothing. The result remains that a woman, however straight she goes, is much more rarely seen in difficulties than a man.

In Western countries, outstanding sportswomen of the past were almost inevitably middle or upper class. Communist countries follow the rule spelled out in the Soviet constitution that states that it is the right of women to have equality with men 'in all spheres of economic, state, cultural, social and political life.' The Soviet Union led the way once it was allowed back into international sport after World War II. Realizing that amateur events were the top sports competitions in most parts of the world, they concentrated their efforts on the most prestigious of all, the Olympics. This practical competitive attitude explains why marathon running is a distinctly new idea for Soviet women compared with the boom that has occurred in the West. In 1984 this women's event will feature in the Olympics for the first time.

It is the rapid rise, however, of two small Communist states that has gripped the sporting world's imagination in recent years. The East Germans and then the Cubans have produced startling talent, much of it female.

Western critics who openly sneer at a system that provides a special school for athletically talented youngsters seem to ignore any comparison with the West's intellectually acceptable ballet and drama schools. Communist countries are certainly biased towards sport to the extent that East Germany has a clause in its constitution applauding 'physical culture, sport and tourism as elements of socialist culture, [for] the all-round physical and mental development of the citizens.' Furthermore, 'The state... encourages the participation of citizens.in physical culture and sport, for the complete expression of the socialist personality and for the fulfilment of cultural interests and needs.'

Their success is not due to lavish facilities but rather an efficient selection process and an attitude that allows a student six years to graduate if he or she wants, instead of the usual four. As Dr Don Anthony pointed out, women improve rapidly when given equal opportunity and a chance to work with men. There is even a theory that by encouraging the population to participate in sport, the state saves money on medical bills. Women get more opportunities in Communist countries, and if they show promise they are helped. Outside East Germany, however, there is little evidence to show that they are still backed when they are less talented.

Some of the major areas of the world's population—Africa, India, Latin America—are a long way behind the rest of the world when it comes to women and sport. For religious and social reasons women are second class citizens and for them sport is a luxury. Most Third World countries expect women to work in the fields and bear children in order to get more hands to work in the fields. Many of Kenya's promising 12- and 13-year-old runners are soon pregnant and lost to athletics. For them and millions of others, sport is at the bottom of any list of priorities in life.

Western women are beginning to appreciate the efforts of Communist women but it has sometimes been difficult to accept psychologically. One of the biggest rows came at the 1976 Olympics in Montreal where the girl swimmers of East Germany (population 17 million) trounced the best of the USA (population 250 million) by eleven golds to one. The Americans tended to be middle-class, 'country club' types. Their opponents were serious, highly disciplined and shy, especially with the hungry newsmen of the USA and Western Europe. To them, 'lifting weights is more important than looking pretty' said their coach. After the young Americans complained that they had been beaten by drug-taking freaks, they must have been surprised by the lack of support they had from the American public. Letters to *The New York Times* asked 'Where is the sport of these Americans? Where is the grace, the self-respect, the humanity? Perhaps the East German women take their skills more seriously and are capable of viewing themselves as attractive, sexual women, not by their measurements, but because of who they are as human beings.' Or again, 'American women do make less tremendous sacrifices to compete and these types of remarks will only

detract from the credit they should receive.'

By 1976, Title IX had begun to have an impact on college and school sport in the USA. Women had their own administrative organization, the AIAW (the Association for Intercollegiate Athletics for Women) which was set up in 1971. By 1980, women's athletics budgets had risen from 1 per cent of men's to 16 per cent. Ironically, in 1982 a decade after Title IX, the male-dominated National Collegiate Athletics Association (NCAA) lured away sufficient AIAW members for that organization to go out of business. Many women wonder if the NCAA will continue to support the struggle for equal opportunity. Too many remember the remark by Judge John Clark Fitzgerald in 1973 when he ruled against a Connecticut schoolgirl who felt she had the ability to run on the school cross-country team. 'Athletic competition builds character in our boys. We do not need that kind of character in our girls.'

Track and Field Athletics
FAINA MELNIK
USSR
Olympic Champion 1972:
12 world discus records

The Sports Cold War. It
was not only the space
race that the Soviet
Union wanted to win.
They also wanted to
overtake the USA in the
Olympic medal tables. In
1968, their women
edged into the lead.

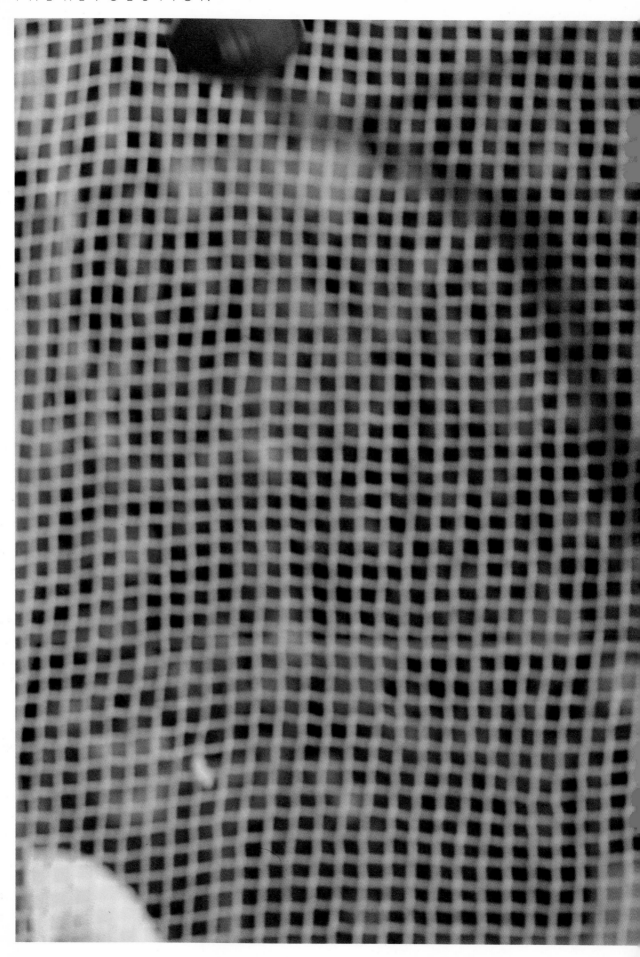

Tennis
**EVONNE
GOOLAGONG
CAWLEY**
Australia
Wimbledon Champion
1971, 1980; French
Champion 1971;
Australian Champion
1974-76, 1978.

The Pro Circus. Entering
the seventies, Communist
countries concentrated
on amateur sport but
Western women found
an outlet in professional
sport — especially tennis.

Basketball
ANN MEYERS
USA
Olympic Silver medal
1976: first four-time All-
American.

An important point. To
counter Communist
success at the Olympics,
the US Congress passed
Title IX (of the
Educational Amendments)
in 1972, providing that
'no person in the United
States shall, on the basis
of sex, be excluded from
participation in any
education program or
activity receiving federal
financial assistance.' At
school and college level,
games like basketball
mushroomed both as
participation and audience
sports.

Iceskating
LISA MARIE ALLEN
USA
Runner-up, US
Championships, 1977-80:
figure skating

Stepping stone. For
several decades iceskating
has been an 'acceptable'
sport for women. The
music and glitter have
linked it to the
professional world of film
and entertainment. Most
Olympic stars join ice
shows, but few women
can expect to match the
$47,500,000 that Sonja
Henie of Norway earned
from films in the thirties.

Gymnastics
ELFIE SCHLEGEL
Canada
World Championships
1978

From Russia with Love.
Millions of little girls were
inspired by Olga Korbut's
performance at the 1972
Olympics. Mothers as
well as daughters became
enthusiastic about
gymnastics.

Track and Field Athletics
ROSIE WITSCHAS
ACKERMANN
East Germany
Olympic Champion 1976,
7 World records: High
Jump

Sport for all. In East Germany, sport is written into the constitution. 'The Participation of citizens [is encouraged] in physical culture and sport, for the complete expression of the socialist personality and for the fulfilment of cultural interests and needs.'

Swimming
MELANIE JONES,
LINDA JEZEK, MARY-
JOAN PENNINGTON
USA
World Champions 1978
(Jezek, 100m backstroke;
Pennington 100m
butterfly)

Freedom. Clothing
restricted movement for
generations. The
competitive success of
the East Germans
convinced Western
swimmers to switch to
the scientifically designed
skintight racing suits.

cantabri

Track and Field Athletics
LORNA BOOTHE
Great Britain
Commonwealth Games
Champion 1978: 100m
hurdles

Leaping to equality. Sport
has not only helped to
liberate women but has
also improved the status
of racial minorities.

Making a splash. Given the chance, women showed the world that they could provide all the excitement, skill and guts that the men do.

Skiing
EVI MITTERMAIER
West Germany
Olympic Games 1980

Snowbirds. Increased
leisure coupled with less
expensive vacations has
opened up winter sports.
More women were skiing
and more spectators
were interested in
watching women win.

Golf
LAURA BAUGH
USA
USGA Amateur
Champion 1971, aged 16

Sexploitation. Although women had been playing golf professionally since the thirties, it took some hard selling to woo the media. Laura Baugh's good looks were used to attract the press, the spectators and valuable sponsors.

Tennis
OLGA MOROZOVA
USSR
Runner-up Wimbledon
singles 1974, Wimbledon
mixed doubles 1968,
1970

Razzmatazz. Professional
tennis jazzed up its image.
All-white dress was old
hat. Designer Teddy
Tinling added sparkle to
Morozova's image with
this gold dress.

Rowing
WOMENS EIGHT
USSR
Olympic Silver Medal,
1980

Teamwork. Rowing is a
strength sport where
women have a
disadvantage compared
with men. However,
there is an exhilaration
about achieving the
machine-like precision of
a successful crew.

Previous page

Volleyball
MERCEDES PEREZ
Cuba
Captain, World
Champions 1978

Swimming
BARBARA KRAUSE
East Germany
Olympic Champion
100m, 200m freestyle;
World Champion 100m
freestyle 1978.

In the Swim. No sport
has demonstrated so
vividly the ability of
women to catch up with
men. Women world
record holders of the
eighties are faster than
men just two decades
ago.

Track and Field Athletics
JANE FREDERICK
USA
Former World Record
Holder: Heptathlon

Women have only recently received much support in track and field in the USA. Jane Frederick's outstanding efforts in the multi-event pentathlon and heptathlon are all the more laudable. How many men could high jump 6 ft, long jump 20 ft 7 ½ in, putt the shot 51 ft 7 in, hurdle 100m in 13.48 secs and run 800m in 2 min 18.6 secs? Frederick did it all in 1978.

Track and Field Athletics
LINDSEY
MACDONALD
Great Britain
Olympic Bronze Medallist
1980: 4 x 400m relay

Sponsored Sport. West European nations organized their national sports programmes often using commercial sponsorship to emulate the success of Communist countries. Great Britain experienced a boom in track and field, exemplified by Lindsey Macdonald, who, at 16, is Britain's youngest-ever track medallist.

Modern Pentathlon
KATHY TAYLOR
Great Britain
World Cup Winner
1979; Individual
Champion 1982

Skating
BETH HEIDEN
USA
World Champion 1979

The all-rounders. Kathy Taylor switched from swimming to modern pentathlon (riding; fencing; shooting; swimming; running) which is considered the greatest psychological, as well as physical, test of an athlete. Beth Heiden (whose brother Eric won five gold medals at the 1980 Winter Olympics) won world titles in both speedskating and cycle roadracing in 1980.

THE BODY

When *Time* magazine featured 'the new ideal of beauty' as its cover story on 30 August 1982, sportswomen felt that perhaps they had made it at last. The article made the point that the taut, lithe body was not only acceptable but trendy. "Abundant flesh and slouching postures have been replaced by a new chic: thin is in, with prominent bones, veins and muscles," says US runner Gloria Averbuch.'

With so much attention being paid to the new look athletic female body, it is worth comparing it with the male, as well as finding a straight path through the maze of myths built up over the centuries.

In general, men are 10 per cent bigger than women. They have longer bones, which give them better leverage and tend to be heavier. They are stronger with wider shoulders and greater upper body strength, which helps them to throw further. They have bigger hearts and lungs. They have a higher centre of gravity and are therefore less good at balancing than women. Interestingly, whereas a man's muscles increase in size as they get stronger, a woman's do not.

Men's strength advantage comes after puberty, however. Before that girls tend to be larger and stronger, which has led to them being more than useful additions to Little League baseball or junior soccer teams. The movie *The Bad News Bears* made this particularly clear. At puberty the female body begins to change as it prepares itself for childbearing. Oestrogen levels and the fat content of the body rise. In boys, testosterone, the male hormone, helps

Synchronised Swimming
ALEXANDRA
WORISCH
Austria
European silver medallist
1981

build muscle and therefore strength.

A woman's muscles are as strong as a man's if they are the same size. However, since most men are bigger and therefore stronger than most women, women cannot hope to match men in sports where brute force and contact are essential. But women can still be very strong. In 1973, Marie McCard pulled a lorry down Bedford High Street in England using her teeth. 'I wanted to prove that it could be done by a woman!' she said.

Comparisons between men and women (if they have to be made) should be on the basis of size rather than sex. An American woman, Shirley Patterson, enjoys lifting weights: 'I'm not really in this to beat men. A woman can't. I'm not trying to lift as much as a man to show them up. I don't hate men. When I go out on a date I don't carry my barbells. And I dress Fredericks of Hollywood all the way.'

Women's fat fascinates the scientists. In general, women have 10-20 per cent more body fat than men. As well as that carried on the buttocks, thighs and breasts (which in scientific eyes are mainly 'fatty tissue') there is also a layer of fat below the skin (sub-cutaneous) which retains extra warmth in the cold-weather events. It is generally acknowledged that this extra fat is used as additional fuel in endurance events such as ultra-distance running and long-distance swimming (in which it aids buoyancy, too). Women don't seem to 'hit the wall' in a marathon the way men do at about the 20 mile mark when the body has used up the stored carbohydrates. They are additionally helped in endurance events by the fact that their metabolic rate is lower. This means that they burn up fewer calories and require fewer nutrients.

However, there are disadvantages. Extra fat means extra weight which must be carried in a sporting event. The fatty tissue of the breasts can pose awkward problems, or can be exploited as Billie Jean King revealed in her autobiography. 'Ladies, here's a hint; if you're playing against a friend who has big boobs, bring her to the net and make her hit backhand volleys. That's the hardest shot for the well-endowed. ''I've got to hit over them or under them, but I can't hit through them,'' Annie Jones used always to moan to me. Not having much in my bra, I found it hard to sympathise.'

Constant exercise reduces a woman's body fat to the point where it is only 7 to 9 per cent (a fit man would still get down to 5 per cent body fat). And with exercise, the 'Playboy bust' is less evident. Since the breasts are little more than fatty tissue, the theory that blows to them can cause cancer is no more than a myth. In fact, where a man's reproductive organs are outside the body, a woman's are safely hidden away inside, so contact sports are not so dangerous.

One of the greatest female advantages for many sports is extra flexibility. Dr Malcolm Read of the British Olympic Association notes that on the whole women's ligaments are more elastic than men's. This additional flexibility, though, can be a disadvantage in certain sports, particularly those which put a lot of strain on the knee or elbow joints. Dr Read feels that if there is one area in which active women are more injury-prone than men it is the knee. 'We tend to find this *chondromacia patellae* injury in which the knee cap is pushed sideways and outwards. It is due to the carrying angle of the pelvis.'

Dr Read also points out the changes which have occurred in the West as a result of better medicine. Whereas 'natural selection' would eliminate a woman who has a narrow pelvis (due to rickets or tuberculosis, for example), now the Caesarian operation allows these women to have children. 'Classically, the women with the wide pelvis survived. Now you're seeing more and more of the slim-line woman with narrower hips. I have no evidence to say that women runners will always have Caesarian sections or that they have a different type of pelvis. But there's no doubt you can look at a number of top class athletes and see they have a more 'male' type of figure.'

It is only recently that the benefits of sport have been recognized by women. As well as the increase in jogging in the USA, statistics show that between 1970 and 1982 women's participation in tennis has jumped from 3 million to 11 million and in golf from 500,000 to 5 million. Healthy body, healthy mind? Neuro-psychiatrist Barry B. Mongillo thinks so. In 1968 he stated 'sports promote mental health and peace of mind... they can relieve natural hostilities, aggressiveness, and competitiveness.'

A recent survey under the auspices of the London *Sunday Times* confirmed, though, that exercise did not produce spectacular weight loss. Instead, as fatty tissue was shed, so muscle was put on. One cancelled the other out in terms of overall weight, but the muscle trimmed figures pleasingly. One 210 lb woman lost no weight despite jogging three miles a day, but her self-confidence was boosted.

The interest women now have in sport is reflected in fashion and to some extent may have been prompted by it. The craze for disco dancing requires a good-looking physique to wear the clinging, shiny stretch fabrics that designers produce. In order to get in shape, women took to exercise. Other designers have concentrated on sportswear: sweatshirts, running shorts and tracksuits in bright and unsporting pastel colours, using new velour materials, can be worn for leisure as well as workouts. The sporty look is attractive for the first time since Lenglen revolutionized fashion in the 1920s. Roller disco demanded more sporty outfits, the all-in-one leotard, the mini skating dress. As Kate Hogg wrote in Vogue's *More Dash than Cash*:

The whole health kick has had an influence on our attitude to fashion. The unbelievable comfort and ease of sportswear has made new demands on the shape of contemporary fashion. Now the shape of the body rules the shape of fashion: clothes show off a well-exercised body; they no longer disguise or contort it. The influence is double-sided—you cannot look good in sportswear-based fashion unless you have the figure for it. The simple, unstructured fashions need to be worn over a healthy body; not necessarily skinny, just very fit. The contemporary heroine might model herself on the energy and athletic prowess of Charlie's Angels, Bo Derek or Wonder Woman.'

Or even better, a *genuine* woman athlete.

However, as inactive women take up sport in the new trend towards a healthy life, many have difficulties. The simple tradition of wearing high heels over a number of years shortens the achilles tendon. This causes pain and can cause injury, even as a result of gentle jogging, for the tendon needs to be stretched slowly. Another problem is lack of any exercise for many, many years. A flabby man who resumes an active lifestyle can often call on a more sporting background than a woman can. Many middle-aged women enthused by the idea of a sporting life find that the simple act of hitting a badminton shuttlecock, for example, is so frustratingly difficult that after a couple of weeks they give up. It can often take a good month to achieve the co-ordination that such a sport requires.

Apart from the simple physiological differences, women have the complex one of sex. More myth and mystery revolves around menstruation and motherhood than any other aspect of women in sport. Women are given sex tests in sport. Originally this involved a humiliating parade in front of doctors, later superseded by a test in which cells are scraped from the inside of the cheek onto a wooden spatula. These cells are examined to find the number of male and female chromosomes and thereby establish the femininity of the competitor. These examinations cause anxiety, additional pressure and embarrassment — especially in events like swimming where the competitors are often extremely young.

When the Polish sprinter Ewa Klobukowska was banned in 1967 for having one male chromosome too many, the Olympic medal she had won in 1964 was withdrawn. It was a devastating psychological blow. In the end she had the last laugh, though it may have been a hollow one, when she subsequently gave birth.

The boom in women's sport is so recent that proper, long-term scientific data are hard to come by. Accusations in the West that Communist countries force their children to take puberty-retardant drugs are thought by some medical authorities to be merely an angry reaction to Eastern bloc successes. They believe that puberty is related to body-weight which is why menstruation is delayed in the elfin-like gymnasts. For years, ballet dancers who have trained themselves down to their familiar lean, gaunt frames found that menstruation suddenly stopped. Is it linked to body-weight, or to the drop in the amount of body-fat? Even if the East German scientists know, they will not say.

Certainly, women who are physically fit seem to be able to deal better with the cramps and headaches that frequently accompany periods. The worst time is often before a period begins, and when it starts there is a sense of release. World records and Olympic titles have been set by women at all stages of the menstrual cycle.

Just as women have won events in the middle of their periods, so they have won major events when pregnant. If they are healthy and fit, they can continue until they feel uncomfortable. The foetus is well-protected in its bag of fluid and does not usually react to being bounced around.

Motherhood is no handicap either. Back in 1948, a mother of two, Fanny Blankers-Koen of the Netherlands, won four gold medals. Britain's top marathon runner is a 44-year-old housewife named Joyce Smith. Also a mother, she is the Commonwealth record holder with a best time under 2 ½ hours.

Early in 1982, 28-year-old Canadian athlete Debbie Brill returned to high jumping three months after the birth of her first child. She immediately set a world indoor record in Edmonton. 'People have said there is a precedent for a baby's making you stronger, but I couldn't imagine it happening so soon.'

The idea that sport is only for the young has been disproved by women time and time again. Britain's Lorna Johnstone represented her country at the 1972 Olympic games. Aged 70, she was placed twelfth in the Dressage competition. At 64, Madge Sharples has become a 'personality' after her peformance in the first London Marathon in 1981. She acts as a starter at races and has enough invitations from around the world to run a marathon a month if she wants. In 1982, a New Zealander Kay Kennett-Low outdid Madge; she was 67.

In the USA, Evelyn Havens was honoured as 'Senior Woman of the Year' by the New York Road Runners Club in 1982. Four years earlier, at the age of 62, she had taken up running to try to fight off arthritis. After seven marathons and some ninety races, one presumes the prescription has worked! Another New Yorker, Althea Jureidini, found that running was too much for her 60-year-old knees, so she switched to racewalking and won seventy-five awards. But they are spring chickens compared with Ruth Rothfarb, the legendary 81-year-old from Boston who is the oldest woman known to have completed a marathon.

There are impressive women in other sports as well. At 43, professional golfer JoAnne Carner, who is older than Jack Nicklaus, is still a consistent money-winner on the ever-more competitive LPGA circuit. In the past four seasons she has won thirteen tournaments and is more successful now than when she turned pro at the age of 30. Swimmer Gail Roper represented the USA at the 1952 Olympics. Now, aged 52, she swims the butterfly faster in 1982 than when she was 18!

The endurance of the female body is being tested more and more. Since Gertrude Ederle showed that when it came to swimming the English Channel, women were Number One, this unique contest has been dominated by women. Canada's Cindy Nicholas set an even greater challenge to the men when she completed a *double* crossing in 19 hrs and 12 min in 1979 — two hours faster than Captain Matthew Webb's one way effort that started off the cross-Channel swimming phenomenon in 1875.

All in all, the glib title of the 'weaker sex' may eventually become a thing of the past.

Powerlifting
World Championships

The weaker sex?
Although women's
muscles are, on average,
smaller than a man's, the
quality of muscle fibre is
the same for both sexes.
While men's muscles
'bulk up' with strength
training, women's
muscles do not increase
in size even if their
strength goes up by 50%.

Waterskiing
KAREN BOWKETT
Australia
Australian Champion:
overall; tricks

Making waves. With a
lower centre of gravity,
women have a better
sense of balance than
men!

Cross-Country Skiing
RAISA SMETANINA
USSR
Olympic Champion 1980:
5km

The farther, the better.
Women seem to have
greater stamina than
men. Endurance events
like long-distance
swimming and running
suit them. However,
their potential is still
limited in cross-country
skiing, where 20km in
the world championship is
the longest contest.

Swimming
MARY BETH
LINZMEIER
USA
World Championships
1982

The X Factor. Women
have more body fat than
men, carried around the
buttocks, thighs and
breasts, as well as under
the skin. Apart from
providing extra energy in
endurance events,
scientists say it gives
extra buoyancy in
swimming.

Tennis
PAM SHRIVER
USA
Runner-up US Open
1978, aged 16.

Tomboy. Girls mature
earlier than boys, both
mentally and physically.
Six-foot-tall Shriver
played on her school
tennis team, with boys.
She only lost twice. Girls
enjoy playing mixed
junior soccer and baseball
in many countries.

Gymnastics
OLGA MOSTEPANOVA
USSR
World Championships
1978

Small is beautiful. Some
critics suggest that
Communist countries use
puberty-retardant drugs
to keep their talented
gymnasts small and agile.
Research shows,
however, that very fit
girls lose so much body
fat that their puberty
could be delayed. Weight
could be a factor, too.
Super-fit ballet dancers
often stop menstruating.

Luge Tobogganing
VERONICA HOLMSTEN
Sweden
Olympic Games 1980

Men may be bigger than
women on average, but
women's smaller body
size means they have less
surface which is an
advantage in sports like
tobogganing where low
air resistance is needed.

Modern Rhythmic
Gymnastics
IRINA GABASHVILI
USSR

Amazing grace. Women
seem to have laxer
ligaments than men,
making them more
flexible and, therefore,
more able to perform
graceful movements.

Glowing. With a lower metabolic rate, women burn calories at a lower rate than men. With more sweat glands spread over the surface of the body, they perspire at higher temperatures and more efficiently than men.

Track and Field Athletics
3000m FINAL
Commonwealth Games
1982

All change? A number of
top-class athletes have a
more 'male' type of
figure, with slim hips.
Doctors suggest that
better medicine means
that more narrow-hipped
mothers survive giving
birth thanks to Caesarean
section. Will this change
the look of the typical
woman in future?

Track and Field Athletics
DEBBIE BRILL
Canada
Commonwealth Games
Champion 1970, 1982:
High Jump

Motherhood is
regarded as an advantage
nowadays. Evonne
Goolagong Cawley has
her child Kelly on tour,
taking her mind off the
day-to-day tension of the
tennis circuit. Debbie Brill
set a world indoor
record less than three
months after giving birth
to Neil, who enjoys
watching his mother
compete.

Volleyball
CUBA v USA

Let's get physical. Contrary to the old wives' tales, women are not harmed by rigorous exercise during their monthly periods. In fact, fit bodies seem to handle pre-menstrual tension, headaches and cramps better. Many World and Olympic records have been set at all stages of the cycle.

Professional Wrestling
JAPANESE
COMPETITORS
Hawaii

Women are tough and
resilient when properly
trained. They can enjoy
contact sports like ice
hockey, rugby or
wrestling without fear of
dangerous injury.

Track and Field Athletics
MOLLY KILLINGBECK
Canada
Commonwealth Games
gold medal 1982: 4 x
400m

All in the mind. Some
people believe women
athletes lack the ability to
concentrate. Yet anyone
who has seen Chris
Evert Lloyd play or has
watched women match
and beat men at shooting
should realise that
psychologically they can
be as tough or tougher
than men.

Roadrunning
JOYCE SMITH
Great Britain
Winner 1981, 1982:
London Marathon

Happy Birthdays! Age is
no barrier in sport. Joyce
Smith won the London
Marathon for the second
time, aged 44. Her best
time is under 2 ½ hrs.
The oldest recorded
woman marathoner is 81.

Diving
BEVERLEY WILLIAMS
Great Britain
Youngest British
International, aged 10.

Fearless. Given the
chance, young girls will
attempt anything the
boys do. Beverley is
actually diving into a pool
immediately below her...
not the far one.

Swimming
TRACEY WICKHAM
Australia
World Champion 1978:
400m, 800m

Catching up. Competition in swimming has become so intense in recent years that women are catching up with the men. Tracey Wickham's 400m world record in 1978 would have won her the *men's* Olympic title ten years earlier!

Track and Field Athletics
CARMEN IONESCU
Romania/Canada
Commonwealth Games
Champion 1978: discus

Big shot. The big and fat shot putter or discus thrower of the fifties has been replaced by the big and *fit* athlete of the eighties, because speed is as important as strength and weight. With greater pride in her fit body, the large Western woman is prepared to go out and 'strut her stuff'.

Speedskating
RIA VISSER
The Netherlands
Olympic Silver Medal
1980: 1500m

Ouch! Contrary to
popular belief, women
are not more injury-
prone than men. Even
the common myth that
blows to the breasts
cause cancer has been
disproved. In fact, with
their reproductive organs
cushioned inside their
bodies, women have a
considerable advantage
over men.

Equestrianism
MELANIE SMITH and
CALYPSO
USA
World Champion 1982:
Showjumping

Horse Sense. Women
seem to be more
sensitive with horses.
With 'better hands'
jockeys can often deal
with sour or nervous
horses better than men.
Women compete on
equal terms in
showjumping. The
women-only World
Championships were
abandoned after 1974.

Skateboarding
LINDA JOHNSON
USA

California dreamin'. In addition to skateboarding well, Linda Johnson uses her balance and flair to stand out at surfing.

Beach Volleyball
San Diego, California

Shaping up. Hand in hand
with the growth of
competitive sport has
been the massive rise in
participation. Why lie on
the beach when you can
be doing something?

Gymnastics
SHARI SMITH
USA
Training

The boom goes on. The extraordinary popularity of gymnastics in the USA resulting from Olga Korbut's influence has been matched in Europe. British official Tony Murdock estimates that, 'even if a new club opened every day, there still would not be room to take all the enthusiasts for the sport.'

Disco-dancing
CAROL NAYLOR
Great Britain

Shake your body. The craze for disco-dancing coincided with the sports boom. A good-looking physique is needed to wear the clinging, shiny stretch fabrics, so women had to get into shape. Fashion designers brought out sweatshirts, shorts and tracksuits in velours and bright or pastel colours that could be worn for leisure as well as workouts.

Karate
KAREN SHEPERD
USA
Black belt kata champion
USA

Self-help. As suburban violence rises, women's self-defence classes flourish. Karen Sheperd is more qualified than most men, having trained in Won hop kuen do. 'If you train four or five times a week for an hour each night, you can get confidence in punching and kicking within five to six months. Two or three times a week it will take longer, perhaps eight months to a year.'

Swimming
EUROPEAN
CHAMPIONSHIPS 1977

Active fashion. With
women attracting more
attention on televised
sports programmes,
more stylish competitive
wear was demanded.
Gymnastics, skiing,
skating — the more
popular the sport, the
more design-conscious
the costume.

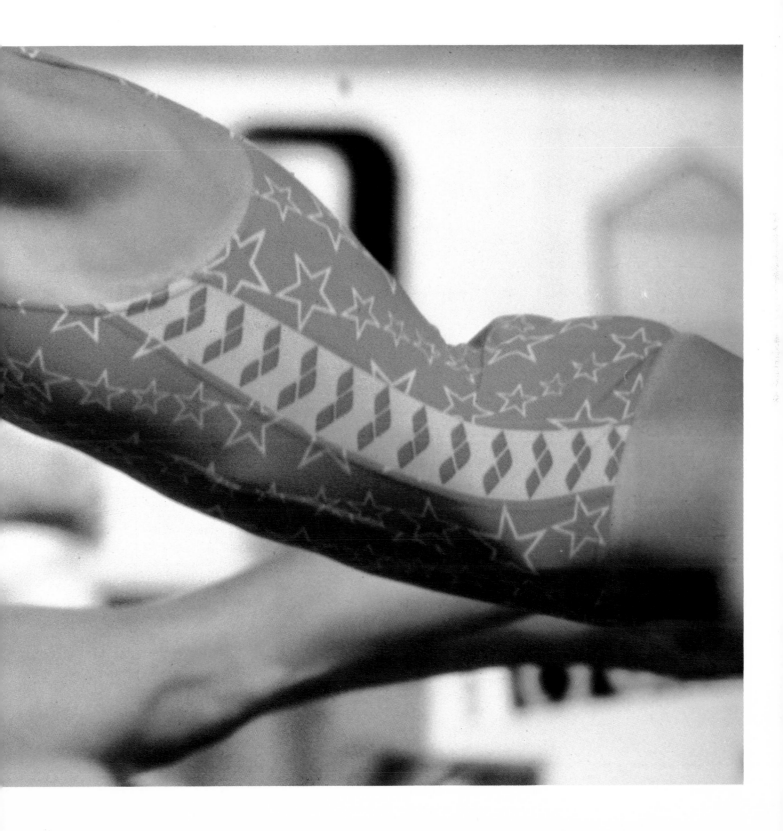

THE STARS

Just as boys and young men have had idols to emulate, now girls and, for that matter, women of all ages have their own sports superstars. The more role models there are, the more women will try to follow in their footsteps.

In the Western world, tennis player Billie Jean King must take pride of place. Yet, as she admits in her biography, 'I take little satisfaction in all the 'firsts' I have accumulated, because all they really indicate is how far behind most of us still are.' As Miss Moffitt she played her first tennis match at the age of 11. In 1979, she established a new record of Wimbledon titles (6 singles, 10 doubles, 4 mixed doubles). She has also won every other major title. For a long time she seemed to be at odds with the system. Until recently tennis was an affluent, middle-class sport, so as the daughter of a fireman she was disadvantaged from the beginning. Once she became a celebrity, she used her fame to battle for a better deal for women in her own sport, and then in other sports as well.

In 1971, she was the first woman to win $100,000 in a year, mainly from the professional circuit she had helped to establish in the USA. In 1972, she won Wimbledon and the French and US championships, losing only one set in all. In 1973, she took part in the most publicized match of all time when a record crowd of 30,472 watched her beat the 1939 men's Wimbledon champion, Bobby Riggs (aged 55) 6-4, 6-3, 6-3 in the Houston Astrodome. In this 'Battle of the Sexes', she 'slew the beast of chauvinism' and in doing so boosted the confidence of women in the USA and many other parts of the world.

Track and Field Athletics
RAMONA
NEUBERT-GOHLER
East Germany
European Champion
1982: Heptathlon

King even invested a lot of her own money (too much in the end) in a new magazine, *womenSports*. (Ironically in the Soviet Union, a similar publication is produced by the State.) Her effort found not so much a gap in the market as a void, though it was perhaps a few years ahead of its time. In 1982, however, a TV channel in the USA was confident enough to screen a series devoted entirely to women in sport.

At the opposite end of the sporting spectrum is the equally influential Olga Korbut, heroine of the 1972 Olympics. Many forget that she was not the best of the high quality entry of 118, but that it was by her sheer personality that she touched the hearts of hundreds of millions of television viewers, on the way to winning two individual gold medals. Her almost reckless skill on the beam had crowds gasping, while her floor exercise, a mixture of dance and gymnastic display, thrilled millions of young girls.

Just 4 ft 11 ins tall and weighing a mere 84 lbs, Korbut had ability as well as charm. A couple of years later, 19,000 of her adoring fans in the West filled Madison Square Garden, New York, to watch the 'Belorussian Bombshell', as she was nicknamed by the press. Although in gymnastic circles fellow-Russian Ludmila Turischeva, who rarely showed any emotion, was the acknowledged superior, Korbut was remembered for the character she brought to her sport; for her tears of disappointment when she stumbled as much as for her medals.

In a country where the cult of the individual is frowned upon, Korbut was never popular with the authorities and was censured by the young people's newspaper *Komsomolskaya Pravda* in 1973. Troubled by the restrictions in her own country and the adulation she received abroad (where she was known simply as 'Olga'), she eventually gave up gymnastics for films.

If King and Korbut received accolades for their efforts in the late sixties and early seventies, there is a long line of women who have made significant contributions to the history of women's sport and it is worth looking back to the early nineteenth century when rules for so many of today's games were codified.

In cricket, for example, John Willes is recorded as being the first man to use the revolutionary 'round-arm' bowling that changed the game in pace and style. It is generally accepted, however, that it was his sister, Christine, who gave him the idea. Wearing a flounced skirt, she was unable to bowl underarm when John needed practice in the back garden, so she slung the ball at him overarm.

The legendary Annie Oakley was, in fact, a real person, 'a sharpshooter who, from thirty paces, could perforate a tossed card half a dozen times before it fluttered to the ground.' She even gave the American language her name, meaning a punched ticket; later it was used to mean a free pass.

There have been other notable female shots. In 1930, 33-year-old Marjorie Foster beat ninety-nine soldiers, sailors and airmen to win shooting's King's Prize, the championship of the British Empire, at Bisley, near London. Astonished that she should be elevated to being a 'personality' alongside aviator Amy Johnson, she told Lord Jellicoe, 'I was just treating this as a pleasant afternoon's shooting.' In 1956, Mrs Leon Mandel of Chicago led all men and women in the history of target-shooting; she broke three world records including scoring an average of 96.9 for 1,000 targets. In 1963, a model, Sheila Egan, beat America's best—man or woman—at the 54th annual trapshooting championships. At international level Capt. Margaret Murdock of the USA was the best of all. She beat the top riflemen in the 1970 World Championships and also took the silver in the 1976 Olympics.

In tennis there have been plenty of outstanding women, though Little Lottie Dod could claim to have been the first great all-round sportswoman. In 1887 she won the Wimbledon singles title at only 15 years, 1p months of age, the youngest winner ever. Known for introducing the volley and smash, she continued to be unbeaten, winning Wimbledon four more times. She also excelled at archery (winning an Olympic silver medal in 1908), iceskating, tobogganing, hockey (she played for England) and golf (she was British Ladies Champion in 1904).

Athleticism combined with grace when Suzanne Lenglen of France set a fashion trend with her shorter skirts. By 1939 even more leg was shown by Alice Marble's short shorts. She played 'like a man' with her Californian style of serve and volley. This style of play was new then, but after the Second World War, all Americans volleyed well, including Pauline Betz, Margaret Osborne and Louise Brough.

Anyone who thinks that teenage tennis stars are a phenomenon of the 1970s should look back thirty years to Maureen Connolly, better known as 'Little Mo'. At 16 she won the first of three US Championships; at 17 she won Wimbledon at the first attempt (and took the title twice more); and at 18 she was the first player to win the Grand Slam. Sadly, when she was only 19 her career was cut short by a riding accident.

Althea Gibson was the first black player (male or female) to achieve prominence and she went on to scoop up two Wimbledon titles as well as two US titles and a French one before leaving the game and switching to golf. Her tall frame and athletic approach coupled with aggressive volleying—like Australia's Margaret Court later —helped make women's tennis more exciting to watch. Just as Gibson was the only black player to achieve any success until recently, so Maria Bueno was the sole Latin American to break through. The graceful Brazilian provided a contrast to the athleticism of the late 1950s, just as Evonne Goolagong Cawley has in recent years.

Swimming has had its heroines too. In 1922, when Ethel McGray of New York clocked 6 min 24.4 sec for 440 yds to break Harold Kruger of Honolulu's record of 6 min 28 sec, The New York Times recorded: 'Woman breaks man's record for first time in swim history.' The distance events have been dominated by female competitors ever since Gertrude Ederle's English Channel crossing in 1926.

In golf, two women were exciting male

admiration long before the LPGA attracted audiences of millions in the 1970s. Joyce Wethered, later Lady Heathcoat Amory, was described by Bobby Jones as the finest golfer, man or woman, that he had ever seen. Across the Atlantic, Babe Zaharias galvanized the women's professional golf circuit after World War II. She is also remembered for other achievements. As Mildred Didrikson she first hit the headlines as a three-time All-American basketball player, once scoring 106 points in a game. She won six out of seven events in the AAU track and field championships which preceded the 1932 Olympics in Los Angeles, where she came first in the hurdles, javelin and high jump and set world records in each. However, she was denied a gold medal in the high jump because of her unorthodox style. After surgery for cancer when she was 39, she came back to win her third US Open Golf Championship by a record 12 strokes. After six more tournament wins in two years she had to give up. She died at the early age of 42.

Another great all-rounder was the Dutch track and field star Fanny Blankers-Koen. Even though she lost six years of competition when the Nazis occupied her country during World War II, she still set world records in seven different events: 100yds and 100m, 220yds, 80m hurdles, the high jump, long jump and pentathlon. But her first world record, when she ran 100m in 11.5 sec in 1943, was not recognized by the IAAF because she raced against men! Thirty years old by the time the 1948 Olympics took place, the 'Flying Dutchwoman' won four gold medals (100 and 200m, 80m hurdles and 4 x 100m relay). She also took five European titles between 1946 and 1950.

Even though women jockeys are now becoming more accepted, it has been a long time since Eileen Joel broke the barrier on 8 October 1925. She won the English Newmarket Plate, an open race inaugurated by King Charles II in 1665. Another Englishwoman, Judy Johnson was a consistent winner in and around New York in the early thirties, but few followed her lead until Diane Crump and Barbara Rubin led the charge, in America in 1969, that has so changed the sport.

In fact, women have achieved remarkable successes in almost every sport, though often they received little attention from the media at the time. Even women's marathon running, which is looked on as a recent phenomenon, has a history. In 1896, a Greek girl using the pseudonym of Melpomene gatecrashed the first ever marathon at the Olympics. She completed the course in 4 ½ hrs. Thirty years later, Violet Pearcy clocked 3 hrs 40 min in London —a women's record that stood for nearly forty years. For daring to take part in a marathon— which she ran in under 3 hrs—Adrienne Beames of Australia was suspended from further athletic competition, including Olympic trials.

It is impossible to list all the women who have performed outstandingly well in the past, overcoming social and physical restrictions. Now that the climate of public opinion has changed however, it is not surprising that a host of women have become household names.

While Olga Korbut dominated the gymnastics at the Munich Olympics, 15-year-old Shane Gould of Australia did the same in the pool. 'All that glitters is not Gould' read the American girls' T-shirts, but the Aussie still set world records on the way to gold medals in the 200m and 400m freestyle events and the 200m individual medley. After that, the silver and bronze medals in the 800m and 100m freestyle were slight disappointments, especially since she was the first woman to hold every freestyle world record from 100m to 1500m. At the same Olympics, Heidi Rosendahl and Ulrike Meyfarth showed the efficiency of the West German sports system (developed to counteract East German scientific efforts) by grabbing gold medals. Rosendahl was an outstanding all-rounder: world record holder for the long-jump; anchor on the winning sprint relay team that beat the vaunted East Germans; and silver medal winner in the gruelling pentathlon. Meyfarth's performance was one of those fairytale efforts that make the Olympics so worthwhile. An unknown schoolgirl who lived near Munich, she won the high jump, equalling the world record and at only 16 was the youngest-ever individual gold medallist in track and field athletics. Ten years later, when all the critics had long written her off, she suddenly returned to form and regained her world record.

The introduction of the 1500m for women made 24-year-old Ludmila Bragina a star. This sturdy Russian broke her own world record each time she ran: in the heat, semi-final and final. Such an effort has rarely, possibly never, been paralleled by a man. This gave more than a hint of the huge potential that could be tapped in women's distance running. Five seconds were lopped off her time when Tatyana Kazankina (USSR) won the Moscow Olympic title eight years later.

Over the short distances, however, one woman in particular stood out. Renate Stecher (East Germany) showed dazzling speed and effortless consistency over both 100m and 200m. Her powerful build, though not unfeminine, was typical of the East European athletes who look masculine because of their strength. Mary Peters from Nothern Ireland was more typical of the bigger Western woman. Obviously feminine but scarcely petite, she has the joviality of a confident sportswoman. Her win in the pentathlon prompted an emotional response in Britain, showing that some good could come out of the troubled streets of Belfast. Later 'Mary P.' as everyone knows her, opened a track in her native city that transcends the religious barriers, bringing together youngsters from Catholic and Protestant backgrounds.

In 1973, an Austrian skier proved that women could reach the top and have the mental and physical tenacity to stay there. Anne-Marie Moser was only 19 but she put together a record sequence of eleven consecutive downhill wins in the World Cup. In all she won this gruelling competition which combines downhill, slalom and giant slalom, six times and crowned her career as the greatest woman skier in history with an Olympic gold in 1980. 'She skis like a man', said one British man in awe.

In 1974 Chris Evert won her first major title when she captured the French Open in Paris. Wimbledon followed soon after and from 1975 she dominated the US Open. Her poise, good humour and almost old-fashioned sportsmanship endeared her to crowds all round the world, while her romance with fiancé Jimmy Connors, who won the men's singles title at Wimbledon in 1974, kept the press happy. Tennis came out of the sports section and on to the front page.

The 1976 Olympics again produced impressive champions. With Olga Korbut past her best, it was an ice-cold Romanian 14-year-old Nadia Comaneçi who staggered television viewers by pushing the limits of physical danger ever outward in the Montreal Forum. Although she won three gold medals she is better remembered for scoring the first perfect 10 in gymnastic history, gaining it on the asymmetric bars. The next day she recorded two more perfect scores, on the beam and again on the asymmetric bars. Even though the IBM computer could not handle a perfect score, spectators understood quickly enough when '1.00' was flashed on the scoreboard. Two days later, instead of crumbling under the intense pressure of the challenging Soviets, the crowd and the media, Comaneçi produced two more perfect scores, on the bars and beam to clinch the all-round title.

Comaneçi had been discovered by coach Bela Karolyi as a 6-year-old in Onesti. Testing her with a long jump, a 15 metre sprint and a walk on a beam, he was able to assess her potential. Like Korbut she had the perfect body for gymnastics: less than 5 ft tall and weighing a mere 86lbs, she was 'all legs and rib cage, with no excess baggage.'

On the track, Irena Szewinska completed a marvellous Olympic career that began as an 18-year-old in Tokyo with silver medals in both the long jump and 200m in world record time (22.5 sec) and was third in the 100m. In Munich, although barely fit after the birth of her first child, she still came third in the 200m. Proving that women can be even stronger after having children, she beat Renate Stecher in the 1974 European Championships over both 100m and 200m. Stepping up to 400m, she broke the 50-second barrier and in 1976 won the one-lap event in Montreal with a world record time. In fact the eleven years between her first and last world records is also a record. A golden way to crown the competitive years of the 'Polish Princess'.

In the pool, the East German girls, typified by Kornelia Ender, dominated the USA. One night the 18-year-old won the 100m butterfly, equalling her own world record and then twenty-seven minutes later, after a change of suit and a few moments relaxation, she won the 200m freestyle. She took five gold medals, overpowering her American rival Shirley Babashoff. The 19-year-old Californian was upset by the string of defeats. 'We swim for fun,' she said, 'I think it's more like a job with them. By the looks of them, they don't enjoy it.'

Earlier in 1976, Dorothy Hamill won every individual skating title on offer to her. Starting with the US title, she captured the gold medal at the Innsbrück Winter Olympics and confirmed her superiority in the World Championships.

There was one woman in 1976, however, who received little adulation for her unparalleled triumphs. Sheila Young typifies the sort of woman sports star who deserves so much and receives so little. At the Winter Games she sprinted to gold in the 500m speed skating event and then, switching from the icetrack to the cycle track, won the World sprint title. This 'double' is not unknown for men, because the two sports use similar muscles; indeed one has been used as training for the other. But to win world titles in separate sports within months of each other is a remarkable achievement. Despite that, few Americans have ever heard of her.

The year 1977 was a contrast of old and new. Australia's Heather McKay won the last of her sixteen British squash titles (in effect the world title) without losing a match in those sixteen years. With no challenge remaining as a player, she turned to coaching and moved to Toronto. There she tried her hand at racquetball and started winning at that too. And in order to stay in top form, she always trained with men.

For British tennis fans, a dream came true as Virginia Wade, one of the most talented but annoyingly erratic sportswomen of the modern era, finally won the women's singles title at Wimbledon. She did it in Queen Elizabeth II's Jubilee Year and in front of the monarch herself.

A girl less than half Virginia Wade's age elbowed her way into the tennis limelight at the same tournament. At 14 America's Tracy Austin was the youngest player to make the top 10, the youngest to win a professional event, the youngest to play both at Wimbledon and in the US Open, where she reached the quarterfinals.

Another American, Nancy Lopez, brought the media and fans running to watch her in 1978 as she chalked up five wins in a row on the women's golf circuit. The 21-year-old drove, chipped and putted her way to nine tournament victories in her novice year. The following season she won a record $197,488 on the LPGA tour.

Naomi James of New Zealand did an Annie Oakley on Sir Francis Chichester by sailing single-handed round the world two days faster than the English knight. She took *Express Crusader* from England via Cape Horn and completed the circumnavigation in 266 days 19 hours.

It was also in 1978 that Norway's Grete Waitz made a name for herself. She not only won the World crosscountry running championships, but she also finished first among the women in the New York marathon, an event which she has since dominated with three wins in the last four years, usually finishing in the first 100 of the 12,000 finishers, male and female.

In 1979, Linda Jones of New Zealand was the first woman to win a 'classic' horserace anywhere in the world when she steered her mount to victory in the Wellington Derby. She was also the first woman to ride a winner in Australia. Then Ann Ferris kept the punters happy on 27 December 1979 when she held on to win the Sweeps Handicap Hurdle at Leopardstown in Ireland aboard Irian by a short head, at 25-1.

The 1980 Olympics, despite the absence of American athletes, still produced women's performances that astonished both crowds and statisticians. The Russians and East Germans made a clean sweep of the track events. Olympic records tumbled but the world records of Ilona Slupianek (East Germany) in the shot and Nadyezhda Tkachenko (USSR) in the pentathlon were staggering. The Russian's efforts in each discipline would have been world records in their own right a few years before: 100m hurdles (1969); shotput (1959); High Jump (1960); Long Jump (1964) and 800m (1955). In the pool, Barbara Krause (East Germany) broke the 55-second barrier for the 100m freestyle. The East Germans produced new names as well, like Rica Reinisch who set world records over 100m and 200m while Ute 'Miss Bones' Geweniger took everyone by surprise in the 100m breaststroke. Straight after the Games, the absentee US team staged their swimming championships and set outstanding times. Mary Meagher carved out a 200m butterfly world record that was a huge four seconds faster than the Moscow winner's. Unfortunately, it will always be impossible to judge how America's other brilliant swimmers—Cynthia Woodhead, Kim Linehan and Tracy Caulkins—would have fared. Only the Olympic winners get their names in the history books.

Nadia Comaneçi of Romania who had dethroned Olga Korbut in Montreal was herself dethroned in Moscow. Now 5ft 3in and 106lbs she had to bow to Russia's tiny Ylena Davydova, the overall champion who showed the grace and vivacity that is an essential adjunct to skill. Comaneçi won just one gold, on the beam.

As the 1980s got under way, winning women began to appear more and more on the sports pages of the world's newspapers. Some make it to the front page, like Billie Jean King who notched up her one hundredth singles match at Wimbledon, despite the challenge of the new wave of double-backhanded teenagers from all over the world.

The next question is, 'Where do they, and millions of other women go from here?'

Tennis
BILLIE JEAN KING
USA
20 Wimbledon titles,
including 6 singles; 4 US;
1 French; 1 Australian
singles title.

Billie Jean King has been
the most vocal and most
consistent campaigner for
equal sports
opportunities in the past
fifteen years. After
helping to set up a
professional circuit for
women, she was the first
woman to win $100,000
in a year (1971). The
gimmicky 'Battle of the
Sexes' with 1939 Men's
Wimbledon Champion
Bobby Riggs is seen as a
turning point in women's
sport. Her convincing
victory in 1973 was
watched by a much wider
audience than traditional
tennis fans.

Tennis
CHRIS EVERT LLOYD
USA
6 US Open titles; 3
Wimbledon, 4 French and
1 Australian singles title
to 1982

'Chrissie' has been the
contrast to Billie Jean
King that women's
professional tennis
needed. Where King is
ebullient and outspoken,
Evert Lloyd uses her
quiet wit and graceful
poise. The first woman
athlete to win a million
dollars, she was invincible
on clay during the
seventies, a decade of
unimagined growth both
in participation and
spectator appeal.

Gymnastics
OLGA KORBUT
USSR
Olympic individual gold
medals 1972: Beam,
Floor Exercises

Olga Korbut's cheeky
performances at the
1972 Olympic games
communicated the fun of
gymnastics as well as its
strength, skill and grace.
Throwing caution to the
wind, she attempted
moves that no-one
thought any gymnast
could accomplish. She is
largely responsible for
the gymnastics boom in
Western Europe and
North America.

Gymnastics
LUDMILA TURISCHEVA
USSR
Olympic Champion 1972:
Overall

With six individual world and Olympic titles between 1970-76 Turischeva had a better record than her contemporary, Korbut, but lacked her charisma. Here, competing at the World Cup in London in 1975, she had a lucky escape when the assymetrical bar began to collapse as she finished her routine. Displaying the concentration of a champion, she landed gracefully and turned to see a horrified audience.

Iceskating
IRINA RODNINA and
ALEKSANDR ZAITSEV
USSR
8 World and Olympic
gold medals 1973-80:
Pairs

Irina was the dominant
factor in two skating
partnerships that
produced 13 titles. She
began with Alexei
Ulanov. They were
World and Olympic
champions from
1969-72, following in the
great 'poetry in motion'
tradition of the
Protopopovs. She then
continued her success
with Aleksandr Zaitsev,
bringing balletic skills to
sport.

Motor Racing
LELLA LOMBARDI
Italy
First Woman to score in
Formula One World
Championship

Grand Prix motorsport is
expensive and not given
to gimmicks. The 'Tigress
of Turin' earned the right
to drive. At the 1975
Spanish Grand Prix in
Barcelona she came sixth.
As the race was stopped
early because of an
accident, points were
halved, so she was
awarded just ½ point.

Skiing
ANNE-MARIE MOSER
Austria
5 World and Olympic
gold medals 1972-80; 6
World Cups

Quite simply the greatest
woman skier of all time.
Moser 'skied like a man'
according to one
awestruck and admiring
British male skier. She
proved that women have
the concentration and
determination not only
to get to the top but to
stay there.

Gymnastics
NADIA COMANECI
Romania
5 World and Olympic
individual gold medals;
1975-80

Fourteen-year-old
Comaneçi took over as
the world's favourite
gymnast at the 1976
Olympics. Cold and
intense compared with
Korbut, she not only
scored the first ever
'perfect' 10, but she
went on to score five
more after that. The
computer was not
expecting this history-
making performance and
registered 1.00!

Gymnastics
NELLI KIM
USSR
5 World and Olympic
individual gold medals,
1976-80

Four years older than
Comaneçi, Kim was
perhaps more graceful
than the Romanian. She
also notched up two
'perfect' 10s in Montreal
and dominated the Floor
Exercises for four years
from 1976 to 1980. Her
first (and the first-ever
on the floor) came when
she needed a perfect
score to overtake her
team-mate Ludmila
Turischeva for the gold
medal. She also scored
ten on the vault.

Ice-Skating
DOROTHY HAMILL
USA
Olympic, World
Champion 1976:
Figure-skating

The USA has a tradition
of producing fine figure-
skaters — Tenley
Albright, Carol Heiss,
Peggy Fleming and, in
1976, Dorothy Hamill.
She had a dazzling ability
to revolve on the spot
and had her own 'Hamill
Camel', a move from
camel spin to sit spin that
had the crowds in
Innsbrück stamping their
feet with delight.

Golf
NANCY LOPEZ
USA
LPGA Champion 1978,
both Rookie and Player
of the Year 1978

Golf fans (both male and
female) sat up when
Nancy Lopez won a
record $189,814 in her
first year as a
professional. Only 21
years old, she set a
record that no male
golfer had achieved. She
also won five consecutive
tournaments to become
the sport's first woman
superstar. Her rhythmic
swing is the envy of (and
should be a model for) all
golfers.

Tennis
TRACY AUSTIN
USA
US Champion 1979,
1981

Fourteen-year-old Austin
picked up a series of
'youngests' in 1977 as
the youngest player ever
to make the top 10, the
youngest to win a
professional event, the
youngest to play at both
Wimbledon and the U.S.
Open (where she reached
the quarter-finals). Her
persistent back court
play, seemingly modelled
on Chris Evert Lloyd, has
earned her a fortune.

Track and Field Athletics
GRETA ANDERSEN
WAITZ *(left)*
Norway
New York Marathon
winner 1978-80, 1982;
World Cross-Country
Champion 1978-81

Rated the greatest-ever
female distance runner,
Greta Waitz has
benefited from the long-
delayed International
Amateur Athletics
Federation decision to
allow women to run
races longer than 800m
or 1500m. Starting as
world record holder for
3000m, she got better as
the races got longer. Her
winning time of 2 hrs 32
min 30 sec in the 1978
New York Marathon
helped the women's
event come of age. She
also went twelve years
unbeaten in cross-country
races.

Track and Field Athletics
EVELYN ASHFORD
USA
World Cup Winner
1979, 1981: 100m,
200m

Evelyn Ashford was the
first American sprinter
since 1968 to break East
Germany's domination of
the 100m and 200m.
Lightning fast over 50yd
and 60yd, she proved
that she also had the
strength to go the
distance when she did the
'double' in the Montreal
and Rome World Cups.
She was voted 'woman
athlete of the year' by
most authorities in 1979
and 1981, but missed the
Olympics because of the
USA's boycott. Her
innovative skintight racing
suit has become her
trade mark.

Tennis
MARTINA
NAVRATILOVA
Czechoslovakia/USA
Wimbledon Champion
1978-79, 82

Just when it seemed that American teenagers would produce enough talent to dominate women's tennis forever, Martina Navratilova arrived on the scene. Playing an athletic, aggressive all-court game (her father was an Olympic sprinter), she had everything except the confidence and killer-instinct to go with her talent. In 1982, her attitude changed and she took her earnings over the $4 million mark — a record in women's tennis.

Track and Field Athletics
ILONA SLUPIANEK
East Germany
Olympic champion 1980:
Shot putt

A measure of her
greatness comes with a
simple statistic. The
poorest of her six efforts
at the Moscow Olympics
(21.42m/70 ft 3¼ in)
was equalled only by the
best putt of the runner-
up in the event! In fact,
her winning margin of
almost a metre was the
biggest ever. Although
she is a big woman, she is
well-proportioned and
explosively fast in the
circle.

Gymnastics
ELENA DAVIDOVA
USSR
Olympic Champion 1980:
Combined Exercises

Just as a tired-looking
Korbut had to give way
to Comaneçi at the 1976
Olympics, so an equally
strained Comaneçi was
pressured by a new talent
in 1980. But it was such a
small margin of victory
that even the experts
would find it hard to put
her ahead of Comaneçi
and Gnauck (East
Germany).

Track and Field Athletics
SARA SIMEONI
Italy
Olympic Champion 1980;
World record holder:
High Jump

When Simeoni won the
Olympics, it signalled the
end of a struggle with the
other great high jumper
of the decade, Rosi
Ackermann of East
Germany. From 1972 to
1978 Ackermann
dominated, then Simeoni
took over. No wonder
the Italians in the crowd
at Moscow sang the
national anthem, even
though it was not played
for the victory ceremony
as a token of Italy's
opposition to the Soviet
invasion of Afghanistan.

THE FUTURE

When the Virginia Slims cigarette company put its money behind the women's tennis tour back in 1971, it used the advertising slogan 'You've come a long way, baby'. Women may have advanced considerably in the past ten to fifteen years, but they still remain second class citizens in many sports.

Kathrine Switzer, who helped to break the sex barrier by running in the 1967 Boston Marathon, now works as special promotions manager for Avon Products. This international cosmetics company has achieved considerable success in liberating women from their traditional non-athletic roles in countries like Brazil and Japan. By organizing mass runs over 10km, 10 miles and the marathon distance, and by offering winners the prize of competing in an annual world championship, the Avon International Running Circuit has boosted the ambitions of women in many parts of the world. In 1979, representatives from twenty-four countries and five continents raced in West Germany. In 1980 the streets of central London were closed for the first time for a sports event; and that paved the way for the first London Marathon. It also helped to persuade the International Olympic Committee that women deserved their own marathon championship at Olympic level. Los Angeles will stage the first in 1984.

The dramatic improvement in women's distance running has been used to make all sorts of extrapolations. According to her husband, America's outstanding distance runner, Mary Decker Tabb, who set seven world records in

Cheerleading
UNIVERSITY OF
SOUTHERN
CALIFORNIA
USA
American Football Game

Do your own thing.
Cheerleaders are turning
their backs on tradition.
American girls are now
asking, 'Why should I
stand on the sidelines and
cheer?' I'd rather be out
there hearing the crowd
shout for me!'

1982, could break 2 hrs 20 min for the marathon. Such a time would be the equivalent of 25th place in the men's 1980 Olympic marathon.

Some doctors think that women will not only equal men but overtake them. Dr Philip Sparling, a research physiologist at the Georgia Institute of Technology, firmly believes that 'we shall see a female distance runner win races in direct competition with males'. This is because the top women are now 'within 1 or 2 per cent of the physical condition of males'. Women's records have been slashed by seconds at a time in running or swimming events where men have been shaving off fractions of a second. If such improvements continue at the same rate, women will overtake men. Some predictions state that by the year 2000 women will match the men in running events from 1500m upwards.

The flaw in this argument is obvious, however. While men have been training and competing strenuously for at least fifty years, women have only recently begun to do the same, and it is only now that their efforts are beginning to approach their full potential. The fact that women have improved the high jump world record by 40 per cent in 60 years compared with a mere 29 per cent by men in 105 years is laudable. It does not imply eventual equality on its own.

On the other hand, as Donna Lopiano, director of women's athletics at the University of Texas, points out, 'The kids we think are super now are going to be the rule, not the exception. We are just starting to get kids who are good already, who have received coaching from the age of 15.'

Coaching is an important field that has yet to be exploited. Women coaches are few and far between, yet as motivators they must become more important as more girls turn to sport. Fitness expert Gordon Richards believes, however, that women coaches have a lot to learn.

Women coaches come in with this handicap of having been 'the weaker sex' for so long that when they're put in this position of power all too often they tend to be over-dominant, over-manly in their approach both to women and to men. Therefore, women coaches rarely succeed with either women or men. They have to cast aside all these 'lib attitudes' they bring to the sport. They do have the ability to coach as well as men, they just aren't used to doing so.

Good coaching courses for women, run by good women coaches with good personalities are more vital than ever now as an abundance of talent begins to show itself. Unless good coaches spot the best of the talent, a lot could go to waste. Just as men coach both sexes, so women need the challenge and variety of doing the same.

This, however, does not imply a brave new world where all sport will be mixed. Richards does not believe that women either should, or always need to compete with men:

On expeditions involving boys and girls of average ability it is important to maintain the social atmosphere while throwing down a physical challenge that both can face and overcome. I do this by designing, say, a day's hike where the girls and boys follow separate routes of different distances and degrees of difficulty in the morning. But then they meet up in order to finish off the day's activities together. I can't envisage a mixed rugby team, but I can envisage men and women's teams training together, especially on the basics of passing and kicking, where they can help one another. Scrummaging together would not be possible, mainly because of the risk of injury. But it could be taught simultaneously. My idea is to be 'parallel' rather than 'separate'. It should happen more often in sport.

Where the two sexes compete on equal terms, there are cases of parity, especially when it is a matter of skill rather than strength. In Britain, the equestrian three-day event has featured successful women, as this is an off-shoot of the liberated sport of fox hunting.

In 1968 student nurse Jane Bullen won a gold medal as a member of Britain's team in the Mexico Olympics. Princess Anne, winner of the European Championship in 1971, was also voted 'Sports Personality of the Year' by BBC television viewers. Her husband, Mark Phillips, who is also a champion three-day eventer seemed to have been less impressed by women's success. 'I think women do well in the sport because of the sheer weight of numbers. There's about 100 women to every one man.

By the law of percentages they must get one coming to the top every now and then.' Every now and then? In the twelve years up to 1979, women have won the Badminton horse trials (acknowledged as the toughest event of its kind) seven times.

In another contest of skill—putting in golf—women should be the equal of men. More often than not, the highly-paid professional women on the US circuit have poorer greens to contend with than their male counterparts. However, the record for the lowest number of putts by a professional is held by a woman, Joan Joyce, who needed only 17 in Atlanta in 1982 and even chipped in on three holes. The men's record is 18. The comparative averages are virtually level. In 1982 Sally Little averaged 29.34 putts per round; Ben Crenshaw, 28.65.

In terms of crowd appeal, mixed events have always been popular, especially where the differences in style, strength and grace are complementary. In tennis, there is rarely an empty seat for a mixed doubles match at Wimbledon, and in 1980 there was a particularly poignant moment when a brother and sister team, John and Tracy Austin, won for the first time. In badminton, women play a significant role under the net, where their agility and speed complement the power play of men at the back of the court. In golf, mixed partnerships attract crowds and now there are even road running events where a man and a woman pair up, their aggregate time being used to decide the winners. The next development should be relay teams in dual track or swimming meets.

Some team sports have already seen the social benefits of mixing the sexes. Some soccer leagues in the USA specify that three or four women should be included in each team. Mixed field hockey has been popular for several years. In Holland, a sport has been *invented* to cater specifically for men and women to play together. Called korfball and looking like a mixture of netball and basketball, it has a growing number of adherents from as far apart as Britain, Indonesia and California.

So far, participation has been the prerogative of the good athlete—the woman who has some sort of background in sport. However, as an increasing number of avenues are opened for women, more women come forward to take part.

As this happens, a greater variety of talent will emerge. In the USA where a lot of energy and enthusiasm has gone into cheerleading, the pom-pommed razzmatazz of supporting the men, girls are thinking 'Why should I stand on the sidelines and cheer? I'd rather be out there hearing the crowd shout for me!'

Although the East German women are renowned for their success at international level, their sports medicine experts, like Dr Kabisch, explain that 'Physical culture and sports have gained a new position and function through a conscious integration into the protection of health of citizens. Simultaneously there has been a shift in emphasis of all medical and social measures from mainly curative to prophylactic measures.' Western visitors to Japanese factories remark on the daily exercises that members of the staff go through, but anyone flicking through a record of Britain or America in the 1930s will find pictures of office workers doing their 'daily dozen'. Fifty years later, companies are giving their employees (usually on the management side) executive health checks marketed by doctors and fitness experts. At last the housewife is slowly realizing that her body has every right to the same care and attention too.

Participation, sport for all, aerobic exercises, dance—the boom occurring in gymnasia across the USA and to a certain extent in Europe is encouraging. No longer is sweat frowned upon. Crêches which are not offered by many offices or factories are essential at a gym if it wants to do business in the 1980s. The bad memories of forced activity at school are difficult to overcome, though once forgotten most women revel in their new-found health and confidence. While the running boom provides the cheapest form of exercise, it can be less challenging after a while. That is why women are taking up sports to suit their own requirements of skill or strength, either individually or on a team.

In the USA, soccer was encouraged at grass-roots level at the end of the sixties. The object was to provide crowds and players for the newly-formed professional leagues. The big surprise for the Europeans behind the scheme was that as many girls as boys took up the sport. It is no surprise in America where competitive leagues flourish. In Europe, where the game has been exclusively male for over 100 years, it is difficult for either sex to overcome the prejudice against women playing the game.

What about elsewhere in the world? *China Sports* in December 1982 pointed to 'a bright future for this sport' when reporting a women's soccer tournament in Peking. 'No game played at the 80,000 seat Workers' Stadium had aroused so much joviality and so many encouraging cheers as did the final match. The spectators had not expected much of the girls. After all, most of them were still in their early teens and the 'veterans' had only trained for a matter of two years. How could they present anything spectacular on the pitch where so many footballers of national and international calibre — including Pelé who visited China in 1977 — had left their footprints? The good showing put up by the girls that evening did come as a delightful surprise to the big crowd in the stands, and to the bigger TV audience as well.'

The emphasis on sport and health in China has begun to produce world class athletes. Experts around the world have been astonished by their performances in, first, table tennis and then badminton, gymnastics and diving. In Taiwan, one woman had already highlighted the potential of Chinese women. Between 1964 and 1970, Chi Cheng, an all-rounder, set eight world records in sprint and hurdle events, and lost only once in one two year spell.

Back in the USA, rugby union (as male chauvinist as any sport) has been encouraged in recent years. Both sexes have taken to it, with the result that some 250 women's clubs existed by 1980. In Britain, where the game originated, newspapers were excited to discover a *dozen* women's clubs in 1982! They enjoy similar traditional social activities, a drink after the match and the singing of rugby songs, although one American woman drew the line at running naked down the street. 'If the men get their kicks from that, it's up to them. Women don't need to do that.'

At Yale University, women started an ice hockey team, much to the consternation of the alumni. Boxing, although touted as a new sport for women, is certainly not. Women boxed in the eighteenth century and it was a demonstration sport at the 1904 St. Louis Olympics.

'New' sports are also benefiting from women's interest. Many enjoy orienteering, the art of getting from A to B over rough terrain as quickly as possible on foot. A compass and special map are used. It is the next step up from jogging or running, adding a mental challenge to the physical one. The martial arts like judo, tae kwon do and karate; water sports like scuba diving; squash and racquetball; even bodybuilding and powerlifting — all these are attracting women because they are 'different'. The mechanized sports of powerboating, motorracing and rally driving have women climbing out of the pits and into the driving seat. Rally driver Michèle Mouton came within an ace of being the first woman ever to win the world drivers' championship in 1982. With three victories in her 160 mph Audi Quattro, the 31-year-old Frenchwoman showed that there is a bright future for talented drivers in the sport. In powerboat racing, a woman twice her age captured the off-shore speed record. Fiona,

Countess of Arran took her boat all the way to 102.45 mph on Lake Windermere in England in 1980. And 58-year-old Betty Cook of the USA, only 5ft 4in tall, weighing 115 lbs, won the World Off-shore Racing title for powerboating in 1977 and 1979. She was the only woman driver taking part!

There are examples today and in the past of women being equal to men and sometimes better, too. However, many authorities believe that comparisons between male and female performances are unimportant. Dr Malcolm Read thinks that comparing women with men has done the women's cause more harm than good. 'It's irrelevant. What matters is what they're getting out of sport, the enjoyment they're getting out of life. I personally think we're heading off in the wrong direction by trying to say men and women are the same. They are *not* the same. Observe kids playing and you can see they're not the same. They play and behave differently. There are a lot of women who would get a lot more enjoyment out of sport if they weren't constantly being compared to men.'

Men and women *are* different and although mixing the sexes works in some sports, in others it does not. The point is that a top-class match between women should be as exhilarating and entertaining, as competitive and skilful as a men's match.

Not all the advances are necessarily good ones. An area that is causing concern is among young runners, especially with the continuing marathon boom. In the USA young girls (and young boys) are encouraged to run the 26 miles

385 yards. Eleven-year-old Cheryl Page of England is an enthusiastic runner who has raised thousands of pounds for charity. Running with her father in 1981, she completed the Berlin City Marathon in 4 hrs and 53 min. In England, however, she is not allowed to run under Amateur Athletic Association rules. Her argument to the leading British magazine *Running* was 'The roads are free and nobody can stop me running on them. The Olympic Games will have a ladies' marathon for the first time in 1984 but Britain will fail to produce young winners. In Germany, anyone can enter any marathon. My ambition is to run in the Olympic Marathon, but how can I get the training in?'

Road running jars the bones and since youngsters' bones are not fully grown, they are still 'soft' and the battering of a marathon is likely to have long-term effects. The magazine editor, Andy Etchells, also pointed out the fallacy of Cheryl's argument about training, 'The young runner's training should be at the shorter distances where the necessary speed is developed for top-flight long distance running.' Certainly participants in the boom in women's sports needs to consider what is liberating and what is just crippling.

Mary Decker Tabb ran twice for the USA against the USSR at the age of 14. Although she set a world indoor record for 880yds the following year, she was plagued by injuries for four years, mainly due to 'overuse'. She was lucky enough to be able to come back to a highly successful career on the track.

Other sports that have attracted girls in the

past decade, such as tennis and gymnastics, have already left their marks on young bodies. Teenage tennis pros Tracy Austin, Pam Shriver and Andrea Jaeger have suffered a succession of injuries, while most gymnasts seem to compete with bandaged ankles, knees or fingers. What doctors cannot predict is the long-term effect of this high level of activity on developing bodies. Will today's gold medallist be crippled by arthritis before the age of 30? We shall have to wait until this first crop of youngsters reaches maturity to find out. On the plus side, it is encouraging that young girls do have a more positive attitude towards sport in many countries thanks to comprehensive co-educational schooling. What girls and boys are introduced to at school has a marked influence on whether they continue sports afterwards. In Britain, only one in three plays a sport after leaving school. This may partly be because some sports like field hockey, netball and lacrosse require a club structure in the community to provide the opportunity. In addition, many teachers baulk at introducing self-defence, disco dancing or the 'keep fit' type of gymnastics for adolescents who find team games and tactics difficult and need to be encouraged to take some sort of exercise. This stimulation is often sadly lacking in traditional school sports. Schools are vitally important in countries where sport for women is not rated equal in importance to sport for men. Teachers' attitudes are so often mirrored by children. As sports medicine specialist Dr Liz Ferris (an Olympic medallist herself) emphasizes, 'If the social attitude to women in sport is to demean, discourage and undermine them, it is hardly surprising that the standards of female performances remain low. Facilities will be scarce and competition hard to find.'

There is little doubt that more women will participate in sport and that the standards will continue to rise as performances creep nearer to the best efforts of men. But 'winning women' is about much more. 'I think what I would like to see is the development of the *family* in sport' says Dr Malcolm Read, 'because invariably the reason the woman drops out of sport is because she has a child. Other needs take precedence as the child has to be looked after. The more that sports clubs deal with the family, the more there are facilities for the children so that the woman can go off and do what she wants to do. Then both husband and wife can meet during recreation time. A husband who goes out and enjoys his sport and the socializing afterwards comes home to find a wife who is angry and resentful about sport. She becomes anti-sport! If she can join in, especially sports that allow mixing like badminton, golf and tennis, then there is a better social atmosphere.'

The liberation of women in sport is only a step towards complete integration, where men and women will learn to take part in sport in the most natural way possible—with their families.

Equestrianism
JOANNE WINTER on
STAINLESS STEEL
Great Britain
Goodwood, England
1975: Three-day Event

Equality. Sportswomen
have a 'can do' attitude
nowadays. They have
won the world's toughest
three-day event
(Badminton, England)
seven times in twelve
years up to 1979. Joanne
Winter was injured — the
horse was all right.

Basketball
Twins PAULA and PAM
McGEE
USA
Olympic triallists 1980:
Forwards

Softball
JANET PINNEAU
USA
Catcher

Pro ball. It is only in the past ten years that women have considered making a living playing sport. Hot on the heels of tennis, golf and iceskating, basketball and softball leagues have sprung up across the USA. The McGee twins, nicknamed the 'Ebony Bookends', are 6 ft 3 in tall with the speed and strength that has the pro scouts drooling. Janet Pinneau won a scholarship to UCLA (University of California at Los Angeles) in a sport that until recently was often regarded as no more than a diversion at the annual office picnic.

Track and Field Athletics
FATIMA WHITBREAD
Great Britain
European Junior
Champion 1979: Javelin

Follow through. Although
more and more women
are pouring into sport,
there is a sore lack of
women coaches. Fatima
Whitbread (the only
Briton to win a European
throwing title) is luckier
than most. Her mother,
who coaches her, is also
the national javelin coach.

Diving
WENDY WYLAND
USA
World Champion 1982:
10m board

Breaking barriers.
Western women have
overcome two
psychological barriers.
First they had to be
accepted as athletes by
men. Then they had to
beat the seemingly
invincible East Europeans.
At 17, Wendy Wayland
did both in Ecuador's
World Aquatic
Championships.

Track and Field Athletics
JULIE WHITE
Canada
Olympic Games 1976

'ParticipAction' - That was Canada's crash plan to involve the community in sport. Spearheaded by Iona Campagnolo, one of the few women Ministers of State (for fitness and amateur sport), the campaign coincided with the 1976 Olympics, held in Montreal.

Swimming
CORNELIA SIRCH
East Germany
World Champion, World
Record 1982: 200m
backstroke

Better than an apple a
day? East Germany sees
its concentration on
sport (30% of the
population participate
regularly) as the
'protection of health of
the citizen' because
'there has been a shift in
emphasis of all medical
and social measures from
mainly curative to
prophylactic measures.'

Sports Acrobatics
XU PEI YU and SHEN HUI
China
Display 1980: Pairs

Number 1 in Asia, China topped Japan in the medal table at the 1982 Asian Games and must offer the greatest sporting potential in the world. Like East Germany, China introduced a physical fitness training program in the fifties for schools and army units as well as 'government offices, enterprises and rural peoples' communes where conditions permit. Eighty per cent of office workers persist in doing sitting-up exercises and other sports during 20-minute work-breaks both in the morning and the afternoon', according to *China Sports*.

Rollerskating
SANDRA DULANEY
USA
World Champion 1981, 1982: Speedskating

Rolling. Women's athletic success is not only helping women. It is also reviving interest in minor sports. Seventeen-year-old Sandra Dulaney grabbed her world titles in Belgium and Italy but it was her five gold medals at America's National Sports Festival that vaulted her to fame. The number of speedskaters on rollers has doubled in the USA in a decade.

Tennis
TRACY and JOHN
AUSTIN
USA
Wimbledon Mixed
Doubles Champions 1980

Keeping it in the family.
In the future there should
be greater interest in
mixed events. The
Austins were the first
brother and sister to win
the title. Sadly, with the
men's and women's pro
circuits totally separate
the only chance top
players have of meeting is
at Wimbledon, the
French and the U.S.
Championships.

Road Running
PATTI
LYONS-CATALANO
USA
US Record holder:
Marathon

Teamwork. Road running
has introduced a novel
male/female pairing. The
Trevira Twosomes in
New York's Central Park
teamed Catalano with
Britain's Nick Rose.
Their aggregate time
took the title.

Mountaineering
LYN HILL
USA
Rock-climber

On the rocks. Lyn Hill is
seen climbing 'The Old
Lady' at Hidden Valley.
Apart from four ascents
of El Capitan in Yosemite
National Park via the
difficult Shield route, she
runs track and field and
won the American TV
'Survival of the Fittest'
programme. A woman's
natural balance and
persistence make for a
good climber.

Water polo
SUSIE McINTYRE
USA
US National Team

Acceptance. Water polo
for women will be
included in the 5th World
Aquatic Championships.
Not so long ago it was
considered one of the
toughest sports for men
with its demands of
endurance and physical
contact. Susie McIntyre
uses her experience of
fourteen years of
competitive swimming to
play defence for the Seal
Beach Club in California.

Judo
JANE BRIDGE
Great Britain
World Champion 1980:
48 kg

Judo is popular because
skill and subtlety are
more important than
brute strength.

Body Building
RACHEL MCLISH
USA
Women's Professional
World Champion 1981-2;
Miss Olympia 1980 and
1982

Is nothing sacred?
Women who want to
take up sport now have a
wide range to choose
from... and they do not
hestitate to go for what
they fancy, whatever the
traditions.

Boxing
MARIAN 'LADY
TYGER' TRIMIAR
USA
Contender, World
Lightweight title

Seconds out! One of the
first women licensed by
the New York State
Athletic Commission,
Tyger has shown that
women can box
successfully. John Ort of
Ring magazine says, 'She's
tough, she's a good
puncher'. She says, 'Its
making me feminine,
more mature. I'm just a
pioneer, that's all'.

Soccer
NATIONAL SPORTS
FESTIVAL 1981
Taiwan

Goal! Soccer,
traditionally 'male only' in
Europe and Latin
America, is looked upon
as a popular women's
sport in the USA, the Far
East and South East Asia.

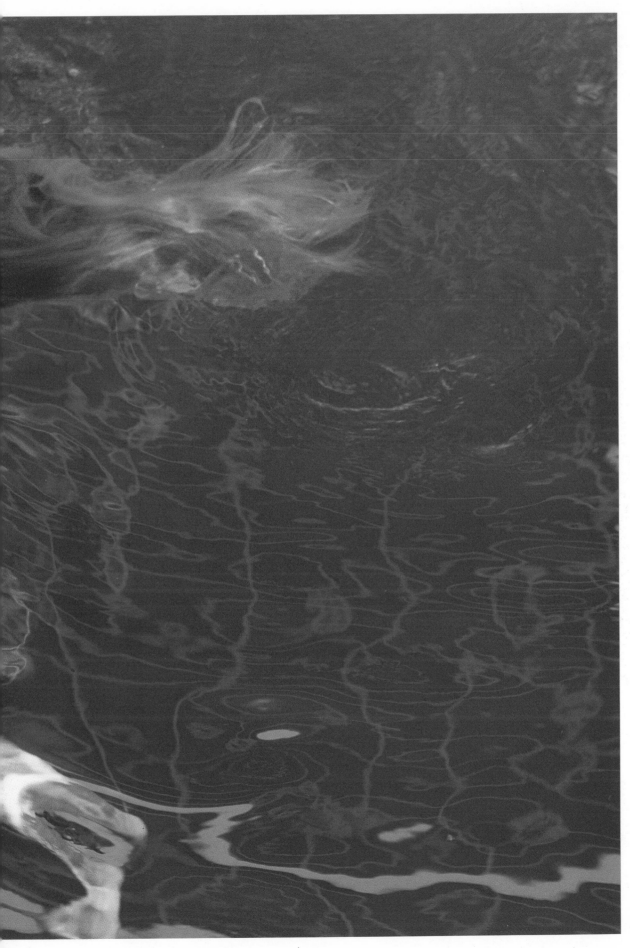

Synchronised Swimming
ALEXANDRA
WORISCH
Austria
European Silver Medallist
1981

Women only. Just
because sport is
becoming more liberated,
it does not mean that
traditional sports such as
netball or newer ones
like synchronised
swimming should be
abandoned. The greater
the choice the better, so
that there is something
for everyone, whatever
their talent.

Gymnastics
TRACY CURTIS
USA

Warning signs. If there is one cloud on the horizon it is injury. Young joints are being put under stress and doctors worry that arthritis may set in later in life. The sports boom is so new that it will be several years before the effects can be analysed.

Badminton
LENE KØPPEN
Denmark
World Champion 1977: singles, mixed doubles

Family fun. 'The liberation of women in sport is just a step up, not the be-all-and-end-all.' That is the opinion of Dr. Malcolm Read of the British Olympic Association. 'What I would like to see is the development of the *family* in sport... where the husband and wife can meet during recreation time, even play alongside their children.' Sports like badminton have a strong social tradition. Clubs will have to provide more child-care facilities so that *everyone* can go and play sport.

Windsurfing
THE SWATEK SISTERS
USA
World Champion (Susie);
World Junior Champion
(Cheri); American
Championships (Lori).

New horizons. New
sports (often without
male-oriented, hide-
bound traditions) are
attracting as many
women as men. They are
setting their own
standards.

Track and Field Athletics
CHRISTINE BOXER
Great Britain
Commonwealth Games
gold 1982: 1500m

At last, more and more
women can turn and take
the cheers of the
crowd... blazing a trail
for the millions who will
follow.